TALES OF MONTHS

"LIFE IS ALSO LIKE MONTHS, SOMEDAY FERAL OR SERENE"

SANJANA & RUDRAKSH KOTWAR

ISBN 979-888569118-5

Contents

Preface

"Poetry is when an emotion has found its thought and thought has found words" as said by Robert frost. I have fully developed my idea through its illustration. As we know curiosity is natural to all mankind. By using this concept, I've depicted my poetry in such a unique way which shows a complexion of different shades. I've use here each month of the single leap year to embellish it more clearly. Here all are unreal, unrealistic, no connection with reality but at some instances it will give a true sense of life. I've use here the birth flowers of each month which will help you to correlate with reality. I exemplified each and every concept which meant a lot itself but we should need an open mind to grasp all in one go. I've constitutes few adventures, depiction regards love, friendship and some with natural elements. I'm pretty sure you would like it drastically.

Acknowledgements

I pay specially thanks to my mom and dad who gave me inspiration to write such bundles of poem. I wants to thanks them again to read each single page more than hundred times, exact number I can't able to count on my fingertips.

I also wants to thank to Rudraksh kotwar (bro) for giving me such beautiful ideas so that I can portrait them into a single piece of set.

" THANK YOU FOR ALWAYS SUPPORTING ME THIS MUCH"

1. January: A full on mystery

It was dawn time, so algid that my whole body was palpitate

I was slumbering on my rumpled bed

Abruptly, the sound of buffeting was getting to be quite arrestive

It seemed that something happened following the window

I was startled, because of this my heart became petrified

Actually this was not because of fear

Something else was happening to me, it was bone chilling cold trembled me.

My lips were starting quiver, I couldn't able to spell out even a word

I don't know what Happened to me?

It was appeared that winter all over the world gave to me.

This thought of mine was uncanny but making me think at least once.

It seemed that she's concierge of this weird castle.

I further descend from stairs to get look all over the castle,

suddenly my feet became froze.

I couldn't able to uplift my hands as well along with the feet.

That old lady came to me to give a slip, an automatically flipped.

The piece of paper incorporated something special that I was unable to express.

'HAPPY LIFE AHEAD' these few words perished my sorrow

Which hard I tried to control,

It was the flurry day in the history of mine,

That day I couldn't forget in

The day in January full on mystery

2. February: I'm missing you

What god destined for us,

I don't know What we would have done,

I'm not sure I try to be happy but for how long?

No one understands, How much I'm in love with you.

You're like a mist, I know

You'd fade in the air

Every night I come here only for you, Then I rambled again When you reinstate.

I never know about you; coz I never meet you

Still I come here again through your sweet fragrance

You're not a rose or jasmine

I know,

You're always seething, filled with unbearable pain

That's what Everyone says,

You know what I think

Probably, I can understand your sadness, the dejection with which you're living yet.

Bcoz, I feel same.

I'm a moon and you're a sun

I know,

I also know this's unrequited love only by me and this thing pricks my heart like a thorn

Since we didn't get time to know each other.

But I don't know how long we'll be apart?

When will I come to you in your arms?

When will I tell you my sorrow and ask you your one? When will we make a world of our own where only you and me?

"no restrictions no sorrow"

But don't know when that day will come? when it comes, I won't let you go anywhere.

It's my promise at once

But until then, I'll miss you and look forward to your arrival…

Your paramour

"moon"

3. March: Is in your Memory at all

It incorporates a lots of things

Either it surrounded with the chirping of birds or in spite the winds in your ear's ting.

It frustrates you at some time otherwise make you feel glad

makes you stiff on your bed,

Chilly winds take the strength from yours

But thenceforth, all of sudden swaddle you in enthusiasm

It seems like a blooming flower gains vitality after making impress through its dazzle.

As we know it's a "month known for spring"

Gives love in its distinct forms which somewhere galvanize you at all,

Sometimes I dumbfounded that the beauties of march beyond the threshold.

Can't be count in tips of the fingers.

Shows you eternal love, not emphasize you into cage

Illustrious moment of snowflake placed misery aside,

Its look like God's promised land from which my eyes not even nictate.

How downright Bizarre this month?

No one even judge its potency

Occasionally it keeps you sway through its amiable environment.

One more thing I personally thrilled in these days,

"THE CHERRY BLOSSOMS"

There fragile and finite nature imprints on my core It ain't just lovely, they represent life itself.

They have their brief life, fleeting nature of life.

But in such a short span goes with deep impact,

We ought to Interrelate its purity with our mere deeds.

It doesn't need anyone,

It has estranged with everyone, think about the true sense of life.

To have fun,

Search for oneself in the profound sea and in the corner full of darkness

Don't know how long he'll do but he doesn't give up

Grief also happens, lasts for a few days, but wonder what it has done in those days....

4. April: all are over

April tranquillity delight my mind

Once more in misted April

Plumed atmosphere, trigger my heart

Willow's solace to lean meanders it is;

Along with creek meandered gently,

Whole world becomes dull

Veiled with fumes,

Birds ready to flee their nests again

For sure, they too wanted to retain their life,

Crows sung sub song,

Others too joined him as heavenly choirs

Awed my core,

The month of peace became something glower No one knew, what'd happened?

Daffodil petal's dipped onto ground

Made nude in a while,

They surrendered themselves in the strident reality Pricked echo, a symbol of upcoming days No one knew, what turn would their life take the hustle and bustle that was there a few days ago now became stunted and stubby day reached utmost climax

subsequently, sun knocked again

allured Dawn valley caught the sight of all

But no one knew what was going to happen to them?

And this happy moment turned into sorrow Right in front of the eyes, the place came under the grip of the sea.

and absorbed the whole, didn't know how it happened?

Only knew that I wish to pause that moment.

But Alas, no one could do anything.

"All are over"

5. May: friendship forever

The flowery scent proliferates all over here

Why not? In the month,

The creation of goddess Maia

The flack of fires deploys onto the ground

To make aura as icing on cake

It's soothing till core, don't know for what sake

Flowers unshackle buds from their cage

They make a new way to stirs-a day

Lean to littoral, stirring my mind

Half a sudden, I went that land

Thought profoundly how it'd utter its course.

I plop down swiftly to precis over that one

Tingling sound resonates in my ear as the crystal does;

I forsake the place, my eyes grew wider for a short

When I saw a cascade in my front

Pour downwards rapidly abundantly

Pearls withered before the pour

Where the dormant bud incline to cascade

Just like the land of pureness

White alluring liquid gives aesthetic pleasing

Nor less than kingdom of heaven

Trees warped over the flowing lake

Minimal gap between them

Seemed like they'd amalgamate eternally Over the course, I couldn't follow it.

My mentality never wouldn't like to aligned until the end

Hereby, the world utterly stop

Not only me, I guess they too want the same

They too want their isolation where they live with peace-

they thought that they'd let this go on like this

Leaves will fall from that tree and will go to the lake and like this,

their friendship will continue to grow when their last breath will come to an end.

6. June: Few more Roses

Your strongest day is standing just behind the door

Let it in;

Each day has some arrogance, come without permission

A charming sunshine diverts the mind of all

Until and unless their mind totally alternate

I've come to that day where prior other month overwrapped

And the coming month swap,

I'm waiting for that time which's beyond my curiosity,

Wants to pick a rose in my hand perpetually

Without any obstacles just wants to find out the glory

God made itself its scent,

Any further delay wants to pick out at once

Numbers are less actually with my needs

Can't count them on my finger tips

Any distractions put them aside

It's time for only smell with smiling

How my destiny pays heeds toward me, I don't know

Don't even want to know

Want this time to be stop forever

This day I never know but today itself I find out alone

Mom said" go to your bed" but

Don't know why I'm smiling more

The fragrance swiftly smites in my nostrils like a drumming beats

Never ever I thought about what it actually leads-

Surrounding world seems for me maze

Probably I've now gone into the worlds of roses again

Seriously, this much huge impact on me are worthless

Bcoz, my mind utterly covered with haze

After covering so much, now you'll find inside me only snows

Even then I still need few more rose.

7. July: you'll be triumphant

New beginnings started from here

Now you are entered in wealthy month of the year.

Laugh aloud, no one here to stop you

Feel better, it's an exam you've to clear

Stop out the storm give you a misery life

Get out from the bed, pay heeds toward outside

Millions are here to cheer up you Starts a new life, put all aside.

It brings cooling showers

Larkspur and water lilies as jolly flowers

A symbol of love and joy

Then why're you still keep your past scars?

Live your life full with enjoy with a happy ending

impel yourself until you satisfy with oneself drastically.

Your consequences would be good really but you gotta take care of later, all are amazed utterly.

This month you'll fly surely

Easily, exceptionally and completely.

After all Your life is limited

You only live once

But if you do it right Once is enough.

8. August: ease my soul

I thought to wander outside the town

To saw the bundles of joy

In the world full of leafy green

Surrounding atmosphere looked absolutely blue

With the mark of sunshine, hovered over it

Walking to and fro into that land

For me utterly peaceful and serene

I couldn't find anyone there except me

no mankind was there have to be;

no sound I heard up to my ears

it seemed like the nature claimed the throne since long years the king of universe, I could see front of mine

the placid sound of gladiolus and poppy tho' hitting to wind

with the gentle oozing of rivulet

the scent of flowers perked up me more which I never thought of;

the warmth of sunshine gave me a different sensation

suddenly I felt out of sorts when remind it the last month of summers

the charming climate turned into lifeless

this thought came to an end when I saw the blue sky with puffy clouds moving here and there,

whirring sounds of dragonfly unfurled

put my heart at ease;

the beautiful day of this month I never saw before

it's obviously the creation of god" I thought"

otherwise who could make this in his life

thank you for gave me pleasure to explore it

I know I can never see this day again.

9. September: bright morning

Morning comes here,

When I saw whole earth wrap with dew

Only the chirring sound came to me Breeze blew softly.

Dripping drop from asters

Symbols of wisdom, valour and royalty

I wanted some few drops passes through my veins

Washed my regret and sorrow at least once again

Blanked mine few times but this on extremes

Swayed from head to toe

Gave an illustrious scene.

I was novice in all these;

Didn't know what was going on?

Only just knew

Whatever is happening, tremendously good.

Such beautiful morning rays was aglow with the love of the sky

Swamped with bloated clouds

No space for rain

Sparkling and glossy light

Made my pupils too short

I gallingly puffed my cheeks to saw my anger

But it didn't make any difference

I stunned with this pleasure in front of mine

I couldn't able to manifest my feelings into words beyond my imagination

It was a gift of god

my eyes to behold,

the land of enchantment,

where dwells the fairy fays.

I was thinking if this is my dream then never break

But it happened

When my charming day turned into sadness

For few seconds I was in mourning

Still I couldn't forget for me such "bright morning".

10. October: being oneself

Day come to give endeavour and prosperity

Granted love and brotherhood

The flickering stars, symbol of this

Trickling breeze rambled towards me;

Crimson flowers swayed my mood

Their utmost beauty winked into the aura

The sorrow, regret coming together hovers in air again

Peace now we get all over anew- Glimpse from eyes widen out at once

When saw marigold and cosmos thrive in full sun

Colourful annuals blossom in our hearts

Either its night or day

It blooms like a fairy fay

Be it October unto the next one

Your scent spread from heart to toe

O! fragrance of love never stops for so long

A precious boon, flutters me more

In your aroma, I'd like to plunge for sure

You are magnificent, crown of gold

Home of bees in their busy schedule,

Myriad petals placed together in cluster

I mesmerised with your radiant beauty

your petals danced in jollity without no fear of becoming lone

Live your life delightfully unto the snows come

Windy loops set on my feet after his defeat

God's creation in laurels of;

It's from wilting of sun

Feed like mom and never stop at once

Proudly a motherly love

It's not the beginning but the end here starts

Garland of marigolds or a thorny rose No difference in them, alas!

Every flower sooner or later wither at last

No matter how much we care of them Only they belong to themselves.

11. November: leafless tree

A bare tree without leaves stood in the cold wavy winds

woeful, on the tree who stood there,

the whole was covered with snowflakes

was all alone my heart fluttered in mourning

It's a home for withered winter in this wide,

only wintery solitudes

Then I saw the little cold birds

who was going there.

Hey! Birds come here

a leafless tree grows there

Unfortunately! Would be no shades

Not even a fruits as well.

Hey! Birds come here

Only a lifeless tree survives there

isn't your perch

Your life would snatch there.

Hey! Birds come here

Stay here for whole the winters

Grasp all the sunshine

Then again go back there.

Hey! Little weening snow Birds come here

Until his leaves become thick

let him wait for the right time,

leave quickly

" o! my little cold birds come here "

12. December: last but not least!

sometimes in December

when sun arises late

up to this much height

sun's light percolates.

There a light falls from sky

Indicates the love toward nature

a cascade falls from two dawn valley

When he tried to reverse his action

He fails to Sow the immense illustrious beauty

Journey towards its end, create obstacles in mind

Suddenly a butterfly came to appear

A lone bundle of beauty

Wandering from here and there

In hope to find his destiny

But she didn't understand when

Her destiny goes away,

It's the mark of patience and change

Touched on camellia through proboscis

all goes in vein,

She sucked its juices

but she failed Alternately did the same.

Wallowing in his fav place

to restrict her mind from grief

Whether she pretty sure or unfamiliar.

Cherished scent unfurled there as the dawn of entity

Her fired eyes, the symbol

She can transform her world

And give way to new beginnings.

Her lane's distinct from our humans

the course she takes from nascent we can't imagine

life is beautiful, full of fun

but how to live we should learn from her

It will always go on like this,

it will never ever have ceased; this is the aspect of life.

"Last but not Least"

9 798885 691185

Printed by Libri Plureos GmbH in Hamburg,
Germany